The Bible

A book with lots of books

In the same way that TV shows like *Brooklyn 99*, *How I Met Your Mother*, or *Friends* have an overarching story told by lots of shorter stories, so too is the Bible one big story in various episodes. Unlike TV show episodes, however, each book of the Bible is distinct and different in the way it is written, often with different characters, and highlighting different themes or ideas. Some books reveal how utterly different God is to us, others reveal how He chooses to interact with us, and others show us how we are to relate to God. The first section of the Bible (the Old Testament) covers a huge period of time and many different civilisations, and the second section (the New Testament) focuses on the one hundred years from Jesus' birth to the growth of the first Christian communities in and around the modern-day Middle East.

Finding things in the Bible

Bible references use the name of the book, then chapter, then verse. For example, to find Mark 1:15, locate the book of Mark (most Bibles should have a contents page), and a large print number 1. Following this there should be various numbered sentences, one of which will be sentence 15.

How to use this publication

This booklet is designed to get you started reading the Bible each day, for the first 14 days. Reading the Bible and praying on a daily basis is a big part of our faith, and most Christians start the day by doing so. This booklet will give you a reading to do each day, a bit of explanation about the passage, and then something to pray for. Follow it in order - read the Bible passage first, then the explanation, then the prayer. The booklet starts in the New Testament focussing on Jesus, and then later on looks at some passages from the Old Testament.

Praying

When you pray, don't worry about what words to use or the prayers being too short, just say what you mean as best as you can explain. God knows what you mean, and long or cleverly-worded prayer doesn't make you a 'better' Christian. Try something like this:

'Jesus, thank you that I can pray to you, and thank you for making it possible for me to know you personally. Please help me to live in a way which pleases you, and give me all I need to do it. Help me read the Bible and understand it. This world is so far from how you would have it be, so I pray you'd use me to make a real difference. Thank you God. Amen.'

Mark 1:14-15

Jesus is King

•

This passage starts by saying John (often called 'John the Baptist', who was one of the first people to believe in Jesus) had been put in prison. Jesus, who would have been about thirty years old at this time, starts gathering a crowd around Him to tell them what the Bible calls 'good news'. Jesus says that those listening should have a moment of realisation that 'the Kingdom' is here. By this, Jesus is saying that there is a different way to live - like stepping from one country (or 'Kingdom') into a different one. This is good news because the new country (the Kingdom) is so much better than the last. This kingdom has a king, and that King is Jesus. Therefore Jesus says we are to 'repent', which means to turn away from our old way of living and 'believe', which means to live knowing that Jesus is our king. These are not physical kingdoms or countries which Jesus is talking about, but rather different cultures. Jesus says to us, through the Bible, to give up our old culture and understanding of the world we've been born into and to start living in His culture and seeing the world His way.

•

Thank God that He has shown you there is a different way to live, and that the new way means you can call Him your king. Acknowledge that the way you're living now will change if and when He asks you to change it. Ask Him to help you live under His kingship, and make Him in charge of your life. John was put in prison - pray that God would help all those beaten, imprisoned, and killed for believing in Jesus.

Day 2

Mark 8:34-38

Jesus is the Master

•

Jesus makes clear here that to follow Him means to be a 'disciple', which means 'apprentice'. Just as an apprentice learns from a master, so too do we learn from Jesus. We read His stories in the Bible, worship together at church, and talk about our faith. Jesus says we must 'deny ourselves', meaning that we don't just do whatever we want with our bodies, time, or money, but rather we do what Jesus did. Your faith, whilst immensely personal, is not private. Because our faith is not private, we discuss it with others - and learn from others who are fellow disciples of Jesus. Whilst it might be scary, we live like Jesus by being open and honest with everyone that God is in charge of our lives. The best way to do this is to find a church (for more advice on this see the back of this booklet). The phrase 'adulterous generation' is here using a picture of God and people being in a marriage, and people being unfaithful to God. Through growing in faith together at Church we stay faithful to God. Later on in this passage, Jesus describes Himself as the 'Son of Man', and whilst this means many things, one of the important meanings is that He was born on earth and lived a human life. He knows what it is like to be human - to be worried, happy, scared, or excited.

•

Thank Jesus that He knows what it is like to be human, and that He knows what is going on in your life. Talk to Him about how you are feeling about telling other people you're now one of His followers. Ask Him to give you confidence to talk to other people about Him and go to church. If you want to give Him your life so that you may have a better life, tell Him.

Day 3

Mark 10:46-52

Jesus Heals

•

This is one of many stories where Jesus heals someone. If you flick through the biographies of Jesus (Matthew, Mark, Luke, and John), there are a lot of healings from various illnesses. Here Jesus comes into a city and a man called Bartimaeus, who has probably been blind from birth and therefore has no way to earn money other than beg, hears about His arrival. In the Jewish culture at that time physical illness was seen as a consequence of either your sin (immorality), or your parents' sin. Jesus makes clear elsewhere that this is not the case (John 9: 2-3), and demonstrates this by calling Bartimaeus and healing him. Notice that the crowd try to shut the man up (presumably because they think Jesus is too good or busy to help someone who has sinned), but Jesus stops the crowd and makes them all wait for Bartimaeus. Furthermore, Jesus sends over some of His followers to go and help the man up. He uses His influence over the crowd to care for the blind man begging by the roadside. There are very few, if any, influential people who have crowds following them around who use that power to care for people no one else likes. What distinguishes Jesus from anyone else, however, is that He has the power to heal Bartimaeus, and by so doing lifts him out of poverty all together.

•

Thank Jesus that He cares for people that no-one else likes, or thinks of as unworthy and sinful. If you have any illnesses or injuries, ask Him to heal them, just as He did with Bartimaeus. Ask Him to make you aware of any people who you consider to be unworthy of Jesus, and pray that He challenge those preconceptions - just like He did by sending members of the crowd over to Bartimaeus.

Day 4

Mark 14:53-65

Jesus is God

•

It was the Jewish people's custom at the time to run their own legal system in parallel with the Roman legal system. The religious court (called Sanhedrin) would deal with all matters relating to the Jewish faith, and so Jesus is brought before them. The charges against Him are not specific at first, they're just looking for a way to kill Him (see verses 55 & 56), but they then ask Him if He is the Messiah - meaning 'chosen one'. The Jewish people were waiting for a Messiah (a saviour), one who was sent by God to rescue the Jews. Jesus tells them He is this Messiah, but then goes further and claims to actually be God. This is a remarkable claim, but given that Jesus has healed people, alleviated suffering, and explained the Old Testament (the Jewish scriptures) in a way that no-one has ever experienced before, people are starting to believe it. Furthermore, when He is crucified and then brought back to life in the coming chapters it becomes very clear that He is much more than just another prophet or teacher. However, for the high-priests Jesus is just a man claiming to be God and so He is charged with blasphemy (speaking in a way which causes offence to God). Ironically, by killing Him they lay the groundwork for the resurrection which proves that He is indeed God, and leads many people at the time to believe in and begin to follow Jesus - as He appears to them after He is resurrected.

•

Thank Jesus for living on the earth so that we can know who God is, and for being willing to be tried and killed so that we could be in relationship with Him. Pray for those who are facing unjust legal systems, just like Jesus was. Ask God to show you how you can live more patiently and kindly towards other people today, as Jesus does in this passage, even if they are unfair or biased towards you.

Day 5

Mark 15:1-15

Jesus Takes Our Place

•

The Jewish council tie Jesus up and hand him over to the Romans, who have the authority to kill Him, and yet there is a custom around at the time where one prisoner would be set free at this time of year. Pilate - the Roman official in charge of the region - asks the crowds who he should release, and (unsurprisingly) they do as they are told by their chief priests and demand that Barabbas be released and Jesus crucified. Barabbas gets off the hook even though he did commit a crime, and Jesus is crucified even though He did not. Pilate cannot release both because someone in this situation has to be crucified. By being crucified, Jesus sets Barabbas free. Just like Barabbas, we have all done wrong - in this passage he represents every human, his name (Bar-abbas) literally means 'son of father', or 'a man who has a father'. That is everyone regardless of whether we have a relationship with him, there is a man somewhere by whom we were conceived - our biological father. In the same way as Jesus sets Barabbas free, he sets us free today. We deserve punishment for what we have done wrong, yet Jesus bears this punishment for us. He dies in our place, and therefore the life we live is one that He has given us.

•

Thank Jesus that He took your place and bore your sin and wrongdoing so that you could have a life free from guilt and shame. Pray for others in your life that feel guilt and shame, asking that they would know the freedom from these feelings that Jesus brings. Thank God for the Bible which shows us how we can be free. Ask God to help you live the free life he has given you well.

Day 6

Mark 15:16-39

Jesus Dies in Our Place

•

This is a brutal and very honest account of what happened during the process of Roman crucifixion. It was a horrific punishment, and often followed a beating (recorded here in verses 16-20). During this beating there is a particular hatred shown towards Jesus which reveals to us just how much He would endure in order to take the place of Barabbas and therefore (as we saw yesterday) all of us. The soldiers also mockingly pretend to worship him, which is ironic and almost painful to read, because we know that they truly should have been worshipping him - not just pretending. They then crucify Him by driving nails through His limbs - long pieces of iron would have been roughly hammered through between the bones in his wrists and through his feet - about where the laces are tied on a pair of shoes. All the while they are insulting Him, as they lift the cross up off the ground so that Jesus' body is hanging off the cross, held on with just these nails. Not only is Jesus in the utmost physical pain, but he experiences in that moment utter abandonment and forsakenness, which is the state that our sin puts us in. He cries out to God asking why God has abandoned Him - and this is the final thought in His mind as he dies. Jesus endured this separation with God so that we don't have to. Through believing in Jesus we are saved from the abandonment he experienced on the cross in our place. Notice that when a centurion (Roman soldier) sees Jesus die he goes from mock worship to true worship.

•

Thank Jesus that he endured separation from God so that we could know the love of God. Tell Him what you are suffering, with the knowledge that He has suffered and therefore knows how you're feeling. Say sorry to Him for the times that your life has not been a good way to live. Thank Him that because He died any sin or guilt from this old life also dies.

Day 7

Mark 15:42-16:8

Jesus Comes Back to Life

•

A man called Joseph from a place called Arimathea comes to Pilate and asks for the body of Jesus. Pilate checks that Jesus is dead and then releases the dead body to Joseph, who does the usual thing for the time and wraps it in linen cloth and then places it a tomb. All this was Jewish custom, as was rolling a large, and therefore heavy, stone over the entrance. When that day comes to an end and the next day begins, some women (two called Mary, one called Salome) bring herbs and spices to pour over Jesus body - another Jewish burial custom. They find, however, that Jesus is not there, and that a young man dressed all in white is sitting near the grave telling them that Jesus has come back to life! It would have been as unlikely for them at the time as it is for us now. Yet by coming back to life Jesus shows how death does not bind Him. Yesterday in the prayer section I mentioned that sin and guilt die with Jesus, and the good news is that Jesus leaves them in the grave. Therefore when we believe in Jesus and are baptised as Christians something remarkable happens. Our old life (the way we were living before we became Christians) dies, and our new life (a Christian life of following Jesus) begins. Just as Jesus came back to life we also will one day come back to life when we die. This 'new life' begins now and then continues in heaven.

•

Thank Jesus that He died for you and then came back to life meaning that you could have life! Ask God to show you what this new life looks like, and wait to see if you have any thoughts that come to mind about what might change in your life to live more like Jesus. If they do, ask God to help you make those changes. Pray for God to help your family and friends, and ask Him to give them the same new life he has given you.

A quick note at this point

You've been following Jesus for a week and have been reading all about Him. That's amazing! If you have not done so already, it's really important that you find a Church to be part of. We'll read more about the Church in the coming days, as we read the story of how Jesus' followers started meeting, eating, and praying together, which is what the Church continues to do today. Your official entrance into the Church starts with Baptism - so start talking to whoever leads your Church about that. If you've been going along to Church with a friend, get their help and advice in starting to be more involved in the Church.

This next week we will start looking at more than one passage from the Bible at a time, one from the Old Testament and then one from the New Testament. Read in the order that they are listed, and then read the notes in this booklet. For example on day 8 read the bit from the book of Acts first, and then the bit from the book of Joel second. It might be helpful to use a couple of bookmarks to find both these passages before you begin so that you don't get distracted finding the next passage.

Day 8
Acts 2:1-16
Joel 2:28-32
God Sends the Holy Spirit

•

We pick up the story again about five weeks on from where we left off with Jesus coming back to life (often referred to as 'the resurrection'). You can read what happened recorded in Luke 24 (the whole chapter) and then Acts 1: 1-11. In summary Jesus meets his disciples and hangs out with them for a while, and quite a few people see Him out and about. During this time everyone is a bit confused about what to do next, but Jesus just tells them to wait in the city of Jerusalem for something big to happen. He then leads them out into the countryside and is physically taken up from the earth into heaven. His disciples then return to Jerusalem and begin to wait in a house together, and then the events of Acts 2: 1 start to unfold.

All those who had been learning from Jesus (called the disciples) had been praying and waiting for the big event that Jesus had promised. A wind (sent by God) then blows through the house and flames rest on their heads. The Bible teaches that the wind and flames are the Holy Spirit, who is from God and is indeed God Himself. The disciples head out into the streets where lots of people from many different areas of the country are. These people would have all spoken different languages, but the disciples

begin to preach of what Jesus has been doing in all these dialects and languages. This understandably surprises people because these local languages aren't known outside of where they are commonly used - a bit like Welsh or Cornish. Some people are amazed and don't understand how this is happening. Other people think that the disciples are all drunk. The disciples explain that the reason they're suddenly speaking lots of different languages is because the Spirit of God (the Holy Spirit) has come to them. This was spoken about in the writing from Joel, in which God promises that He will send his Holy Spirit. The book of Joel was written hundreds of years before the events of the book of Acts, and so therefore it was 'prophetic', that is, that it told what was going to happen before it actually happened. There are lots of prophecies written about Jesus and what he would do. Therefore all the people (who would have been Jews who knew this prophecy) are amazed at what is happening - because it is what they've been waiting for. Later on in chapter 2 of Acts (verse 41), it is recorded that about 3000 people started believing in Jesus and therefore these men, women, and children were baptised that day.

Thank God for sending the Holy Spirit so that the disciples could tell everyone - regardless of their language - about who Jesus was. Ask God to give you the Holy Spirit so that you can live as a Christian. Wait in silence for a few moments, inviting the Holy Spirit (who is God) to come into your life. Thank God for the prophecy book of Joel, written hundreds of years before Jesus, which teaches us about how to live. Think of a couple of your friends who might want to know about Jesus and pray that God would give you a chance to tell them about Him.

Day 9

Acts 2:42-47
Psalm 100

God's People Live in Community

•

The book of Acts is an account of the first Christians, who started meeting together in Jerusalem in about 33 AD and soon spread out across the Middle East. This is a description of how those first Christians lived. A few key things to pick up from this passage are that, firstly, they were keen to hear the apostles' (the first Bishops/church leaders) teaching, and therefore lived by this teaching. A summary of what the apostles taught (called the apostles creed) can be seen at the back of the booklet. This is still used by Christians today to guide our beliefs. Secondly, the bible says they were in 'fellowship' with one another - meaning they were deeply caring about every aspect of each other's lives. Thirdly, they broke bread, meaning they shared bread and wine as a way of remembering, reliving, and participating in the meal that Jesus shared with his disciples. Lastly, they spent time in prayer together.

Their community therefore shared everything, cared for anyone in need, and seemed to be having a pretty great time! Verse 47 says they were praising God and enjoying getting on with everyone in their lives. No wonder therefore that people were joining this group - the first Church - on a daily basis. The Psalms are very old (long before the early church) and would have been used as the songbook of Jewish worship in the time of the first Christians. Psalm 100 would have been one of the Psalms they used to praise God - to tell Him how great He is.

•

Read Psalm 100 out loud as a way of praising God. Think about the words, and what it says about the power, kindness, and glory of God. Thank God that you can pray to Him. Ask Him to use you in the Church to care for those in need, and to help you to learn from other Christians and help other Christians in their faith. If you know that someone is upset, hurt, or struggling then pray for them.

Exodus 12:1-10
John 1:29-34

God Gives Freedom

•

Today we're starting to unpack some of the story that comes long before Jesus. The community of people who worshipped God in the Old Testament have so far been referred to in this booklet as 'the Jews'. This is kind of correct, but also oversimplified. God had made Himself known to a man named Abraham who was living in the Middle East about 2,000 years before Jesus. Abraham had a family who kept on growing (over many generations) until they were basically a huge community of people who were collectively referred to as 'Israel'. These people had all moved into Egypt to escape poverty (very much like modern day migrants), but over the course of 300 years they went from being guests in the country to slaves of the native Egyptians. Two men (called Moses and Aaron) were chosen to lead these people to freedom and out of slavery. They spend months trying to talk the leader of Egypt - Pharaoh - into releasing all the slaves, but he doesn't go for it. This greatly angers God, who hates oppression and injustice. Therefore He sends various punishments on Egypt to both demonstrate his love for Israel and also to express His hatred of oppression.

We pick up the story where Pharaoh still refuses to let the slaves go, and so God sends death upon the first born child in every family. He commands Israel - his chosen people - to sacrifice a lamb and mark their homes with its blood before eating it. Then the people have pleased God (because by sacrificing a lamb they are showing that God is worth more to them - a lamb would have been a vast expense), and they also, therefore, are protected from God's anger. When God kills the firstborn in each family, they are protected by the blood of this lamb. This is what Jesus does for us today - as the text in John makes clear. Jesus is the lamb that takes away sin, and therefore protects us from God's righteous anger and the way we live when we don't honour Him.

Thank God for sending Jesus so that we can be free. Tell him anything that you feel is weighing you down at the moment - maybe it is worry, fear, anxiety, guilt, or hopelessness. Ask Him to give you freedom from these things. Pray for those who are trapped in slavery at the moment - especially those who are people trafficked or taken without consent. Pray they would be set free, and ask God to show you how you can live in a way that helps them be free.

Day 11

Exodus 14:10-28
Galatians 4:1-7

God Hates Oppression

•

Having seen the power of God, Pharaoh the King of Egypt decides that it is not worth fighting against God, Moses, and Aaron anymore, and decides to let the Israelites (the slaves who worship God) go free (Exodus 12:31). A couple of chapters later (in 14: 3), however, Pharoah changes his mind and decides that it's worth trying to chase after the slaves and recapture them. In verse 10 (where our reading starts), Pharaoh is chasing after the Israelites through the desert and we are told that they are scared and cry out to God. Following this, Moses leads them towards the Red Sea and then God sends a strong wind which make the waters part and allows the people to pass through, walking along the (now dry) sea bed. The waters then close over the Egyptian army meaning that the Israelites are completely free from their oppressors.

A theme which is still important today is picked up in the second reading. Galatians is a letter written by Saint Paul, one of the early church leaders mentioned in the book of Acts. The theme that is true in the Exodus is still true today. God rescues those who trust in Him out of slavery and being trapped by things both physically and spiritually. Galatians makes clear that when God rescues us from slavery we are also adopted into His family - meaning that we are given (inherit) eternal life, that is, life in heaven after we die.

•

Thank God for the story of the sea parting so that people could be free from slavery. Pray for organisations that work against modern slavery today. Tell God if you feel trapped or oppressed by anything in your life - maybe thoughts you keep having, someone bullying or being vindictive towards you, or something that you're fearful of. Ask Him to lead you away from these feelings, thoughts, or fears. Ask Him to give you the Holy Spirit so that you can know him as your Father.

Day 12

Exodus 17:1-7
John 4:1-26

God Gives Eternal Life

•

Having crossed the Red Sea the people being led by Moses now find themselves in a desert on the Sinai Peninsula (in between modern Israel and Egypt). They are camping at a place called Rephidim, where there is no water, and so the people start getting annoyed at Moses. They even say it would have been better to stay as slaves in Egypt than die of thirst in the desert (verse 3). Moses' frustration and fear is clear here - he thinks that the people are about to kill him by stoning. In this frustration he cries out to God, who answers his prayer by giving them water. However, this water is only a temporary placeholder for the true water that is to come - water that will satisfy thirst forever, as the second reading makes clear.

In the reading from John Jesus is talking with a woman at the well, who would have been cast out of her community for having multiple affairs, and he starts telling her about a mysterious kind of water, which means she will never be thirsty again. This water is a metaphor for Jesus, and the story of God giving Moses and the people water from the rock is a foreshadowing of Jesus coming out of the grave (which would have been a cave in a hillside). The first passage points to Jesus - it is a sign of what is to come. The second passage explains why the story of the water from the rock was so important. This is often how the Old Testament and the New Testament work together.

•

Jesus says that He is the water that gives eternal life (v13). Thank Him that He has given you eternal life. Just like Moses told God of his frustration and fear, tell God if you're worried, scared or annoyed about anything. Ask Him to guide you as you deal with the situation. Jesus is the living water - meaning that he will always satisfy. Pray for those of your friends and family who feel dissatisfied and thirsty for something better in life, that they would meet Jesus.

Day 13
Exodus 19:1-8
1 Peter 2:4-9
God Cares About You

•

The story of Exodus continues here with a dramatic encounter between God and Moses. Whilst not the first dramatic encounter (that's way back in Exodus 3), it prepares God's people to be ready for when God gives them the ten commandments - a summary of the rules they are to live by. The purpose behind giving these rules is revealed in verses 5 & 6 of the reading. Moses goes up to the top of the mountain, and God reminds Moses of how powerful He is. God then says that if the people of Israel (God's people) keep their relationship (called a covenant) with Him then they will be His treasured possession. 'The covenant' is a theme that runs through the whole of the Bible. It means God's binding, eternal, and committed relationship with his people. It can also be a relationship between two people. Marriage, for example, is a covenant.The reason that marriage is so important to Christians is that it is a picture of God's relationship with His people. Just as God is in this deep and binding relationship (a covenant) with

His people, so too are a husband and wife when they get married. Therefore when two people get married they are a model of God's covenant with His people today, called the Church.

As we will see tomorrow, this covenant God makes with His people depends on them living good and perfect lives that please Him (see Exodus 19:5 - 'if you obey me'), which the Israelites could and did not do, and nor do we today. Verses 4-8 of the second reading (from 1 Peter) are quite complicated in the language they use, but they all point to Jesus. Jesus is the living Stone spoken about in v4. Find a Christian friend or small group at your local church and ask to discuss this passage with them. Verse 9, however, is very clear. This covenant spoken about many years ago in the time of Moses is still true today, only now it is perfect because God sent Jesus to take our place and live the perfect life that neither the Israelites, nor we, could live.

Tell God what you are thankful for today about these readings from the Bible. Ask Him to help you to live knowing that He is already pleased with you - because, as it says in 1 Peter 2:9, you are part of the Church, God's 'special possession'. He really cares about you! Pray for any Christian friends you have, that they would know this today, and that it would positively affect the way they live. 1 Peter talks about people who are rejected. Pray for all those who feel unwanted or uncared for, that they would know God's love for them.

Day 14

Exodus 20:1-7
Ephesians 2:1-10

God Saves

•

The 10 Commandments are a well known summary of Jewish moral law, which showed God's people the way to live before Jesus came along. Jesus did all these things perfectly, and affirmed that His followers should obey all of these commands. The difference is that it is not by being a good person that we are 'saved' or 'get into heaven'. In the second passage St Paul writes a letter which tells us being in relationship with Jesus - being 'saved', and therefore going to heaven - only happens through God's grace. We can't earn a relationship with Jesus by following the 10 commandments recorded in Exodus 20. If you have started a relationship with Jesus this is only because He has started a relationship with you!

Ephesians 2:1 says that we were dead in sin and in the way we used to live. This means that living a life of selfishness and rebellion against God leaves us in a state similar to death - with no apparent hope! However, as verse 4 makes clear, because God is merciful he brings us back to life. This is not something we've done ourselves, therefore we can't boast that we're 'good people'. Instead, we can only thank God for letting us be in relationship with Him. Therefore, because we are already saved, we are called to live in a way which pleases God. Being saved cost us nothing - Jesus paid the price, took our place, and rose again. But following Him and worshipping Him will cost us everything: our money; our time; our lifestyles. But as I and so many other followers of Jesus have found, it is the most wonderful, meaningful, joyous, gritty, hard, and rewarding way to live.

•

Thank Jesus that He has saved you from an eternity without Him, and tell Him what difference you feel he has made in your life. Ask Him to help you live a life that worships Him because He has already saved you. Tell Him what you are enjoying in life right now, tell Him what you are finding hard. Ask God to show you what 'good works' he has prepared in advance for you (Ephesians 2:10). Think about who you could help today.

What's next?

____

There are a few important things which you might have picked up over the last two weeks. Most importantly, keep reading the Bible and praying! To help you in this, why not check out **bibleinoneyear.org**, which will give you a set of readings (like this booklet did) and explain it a bit. Ask your Church leader or a Christian friend for help.

Finding a Church

Finding a Church is really important, as it is where you'll be baptised (your official entry into following Jesus), and continue to grow in faith. Make sure that you find a Church where you can really get to learn more about the Bible and grow in your faith.

There are loads of great Churches in the UK! If you'd like to connect with a Church near you and need some help, feel free to email:

publishing@stthomas.church